LIVE INSPIRED

Live Inspired

A Quote Book

SYDNEY HELFAND

Copyright © 2020 by Sydney Helfand

All rights reserved. No part of this book may be reproduced in any manner whatsoever without written permission except in the case of brief quotations embodied in critical articles and reviews.

First Printing, 2020

To my sister, Alyssa Helfand, for always supporting me in every outlet of my life.

Note from Author

I have a passion for inspiring others to better themselves in their lives and creating quotes is an outlet for me to promote change. I would create quotes in my notes when I would think about them, whether I was going for a hike, a bike ride, or just being with my friends. As I continued to add on to my quotes and ideas, I decided that I want to share them to hopefully inspire others in some way. Photography is one of my other passions and this book contains some of my favorite photos that I have taken. Each quote and photo has great meaning to me, and I hope that you find them as a source of inspiration in your life.

Life Experiences/Opportunities

Everyone has opportunities,

but taking advantage

of those opportunities

is what determines success.

Life experiences bring wisdom.

Maturity comes from

using newfound wisdom.

I am my habits.

Decide each thing you want in life,

and make each one a must.

Know why something must be done,

and you will get it done.

The true happiness

that is derived from success

can only be felt through

hard work and sacrifice.

Success without hard work

or sacrifice is hollow.

Being fulfilled is different

from having fun.

Chase fulfillment,

happiness will follow.

Pain is a signal.

Embrace it.

Learn from it.

Change.

People

*Don't worry

about pleasing others,

just do

what you know is right.*

Look up to your idols

and learn from them,

but become someone else's.

Be with people

that make you feel like

you can say anything.

*It is only when you attempt

to walk in someone else's shoes

that you can truly understand them.*

*Be with the people

you want as your headrest,

the people that will always

keep your head up.*

Taking Advantage of Life's Moments

Time is granted.

Do not take it for granted.

Never regret, just learn.

Sometimes it is good

when you don't get everything

you want.

Life is a series of moments

linked together,

make the moments.

It's not

I WAS here,

it's

I AM here.

You are here.

What will you do with this moment?

Life is not meant to be lived passively,

live actively.

Make each day feel special,

and it will be.

Risks/Obstacles

Risks are meant to be taken,

but not blindly.

Don't hit the brakes

just because there

is a bump in the road.

Sometimes you need to speed up

to make the bump easier to handle.

Even in choppy and unclear water,

there is a way to get across.

Find your way.

Everyone has obstacles,

what determines success is how they overcome them.

SEIZE

opportunities when you see them,

CREATE

opportunities when they are not there.

Challenges

provoke change;

adapting to new situations

provokes resilience.

Nature

I was thinking about why nature connects to so many inspirational quotes. It's because nature is a flow of a natural cycle that we want to connect to. It always continues to flow.

Summer, spring...

The sun sets the same way each day,

but it's the clouds

that change the sunset.

Clouds in life are ok

because they make the sunset even prettier,

but don't let the clouds

block your sun.

Everyone may watch

the same sunset,

but not everyone

gets the same thing out of it.

Energy

Bring positive energy to the world

because you will never know what might come out of it.

*We don't know happiness

without knowing pain,

and we don't know pain

without being happy.*

Confidence

When you meet someone

the question is not whether

they will like you

it is whether

you will like them.

*Confidence is

being comfortable

in your own silence.*

Becoming

Being successful

is not about

what you achieve,

it is about

who you become

in the process.

Decide who you want to be in 5 years.

Start now.

Finding yourself lost

is the first step

to finding yourself.

Forgiveness is freeing.

The past is gone.

The future will always depend

on what you do now.

Love yourself so much

that you keep yourself grounded,

treat your body with respect,

and fill your mind with love and gratitude.

If you don't,

no one else truly can.

You are the

beginning,

middle,

and end

of your story.

The only failure in life

is failure to continually grow.

I am not who I was yesterday.

I am not who I will be tomorrow.

I am growing and

I am now.

Find the strength

in your own voice.

Don't fear

others thoughts.

I became free

when I let go

of the habits

that did not serve me.

Never make decisions

out of fear.

The second

I started living for me

was the second

I became me.

Relationships

To love so deeply is the greatest gift.

I am my most loyal companion.

Realizing that I am the one

in control of my life

is the scariest

yet the most liberating feeling.

How we choose

to spend our time

becomes who we are.

It's your life,

choose the people worthy of sharing it.

Life's most amazing gift

is understanding someone so deeply.

***

Observation

When you're on the top of a hill looking at the view of a city, one can hear noises from different spots, but each noise is fainter. You hear a siren from one part of the city and truck from another. When one is up close they could only hear the noise of the people and cars near them. This shows us how perspective can change what we choose to hear or not. If one steps back and looks at the big picture or the "whole city" the individual noise is so faint, sometimes goes away and blends in. If there is an issue or something "too loud" from up close, looking at the big picture is key.

Lightning Source UK Ltd.
Milton Keynes UK
UKHW050414050920
369327UK00002B/25